# Viola Time Runners

## Piano accompaniment book

### Kathy and David Blackwell

**Teacher's note**

These piano parts are written to accompany the tunes in *Viola Time Runners*. They are an alternative to the viola duet accompaniments or audio tracks, and are not designed to be used with those items. A separate violin piano accompaniment book is available providing parts for when violas play together with violins using *Fiddle Time Runners*.

Kathy and David Blackwell

OXFORD
UNIVERSITY PRESS

# OXFORD
## UNIVERSITY PRESS

Great Clarendon Street, Oxford OX2 6DP,
United Kingdom

Oxford University Press is a department of the University of Oxford.
It furthers the University's objective of excellence in research, scholarship,
and education by publishing worldwide. Oxford is a registered trade mark of
Oxford University Press in the UK and in certain other countries

ISBN 978-019-336620-0

Cover illustration by Martin Remphry

Music and text origination Katie Johnston and Julia Bovee
Printed in Great Britain

# Contents

# 1. Start the show

KB & DB

**Rock tempo**

6

## 2. Banyan tree

C string special

Jamaican folk tune

# 3. Heat haze

KB & DB

# 4. Medieval tale

KB & DB

# 5. In memory

*for Eileen*

C string special

KB & DB

# 6. *Chase in the dark*

KB & DB

# 7. Merrily danced the Quaker's wife

Scottish folk tune

8. *O leave your sheep: page 14*

# 9. Jingle bells

J. Pierpont

Nos. 8 and 9 are reversed to avoid a page turn.

# 8. O leave your sheep

C string special

French folk tune

# 10. Allegretto in C

Mozart

# 11. The Mallow fling

Irish folk tune

# 12. Noël

C string special

Daquin

# 13. Finale from the 'Water Music'

Handel

# 14. Ecossaise in G

Beethoven

# 15. Viola Time rag

KB & DB

# 16. Busy day

KB & DB

# 17. On the go!

KB & DB

* The repeat is written out in full in the viola part.

18. Blue whale: page 26

# 19. Takin' it easy

KB & DB

* The repeat is written out in full in the viola part.
Nos. 18 and 19 are reversed to avoid a page turn.

# 18. Blue whale

C string special

KB & DB

# 20. Mean street chase

C string special

KB & DB

**Funky**

# 21. Ten thousand miles away

C string special

Sea shanty

**With a good swing**

**Fine**

**D.C. al Fine**

# 22. I got those viola blues

KB & DB

# 23. Air in C

J. C. Bach

# 24. Prelude from 'Te Deum'

Charpentier

# 25. That's how it goes!

KB & DB

# 26. Flamenco dance

KB & DB

# 27. Somebody's knocking at your door

Spiritual

# 28. The old chariot

Sea shanty

# 29. Adam in the garden

Jamaican folk tune

30. Air: page 44

# 31. The wee cooper o' Fife

Scottish folk tune

Nos. 30 and 31 are reversed to avoid a page turn.

# 30. Air

**Allegro**

Handel

# 32. Aerobics!

KB & DB

# 33. Caribbean sunshine

KB & DB

# 18. Yodelling song

German folk tune

This piece is an alternative to No. 18 Blue whale (C string special) and can be found in the Ensemble parts section of the pupil book.

# 20. Romani band

KB & DB

This piece is an alternative to No. 20 Mean street chase (C string special) and can be found in the Ensemble parts section of the pupil book.